Hey Asher
This is OSTRICH LOGIC
and you are here.
Thanks for
coming!
Ostri, logically..

Ostrich LOGIC

THE VOICE OF THE OSTRICH

LOU FERRERI

AnimaLogic Press

Dedicated to Hannah and her elders.

Illustrations and Text Copyright © 2003 Lou Ferreri

AnimaLogic Press
1245 Fairmount Avenue
St. Paul, MN 55105 USA

Website address: www.ostrichlogic.com
email address: ostrichlogic@visi.com

Ferreri, Lou
    Ostrich Logic / by Lou Ferreri.
    Summary: Realistic animal illustrations with whimsical, logical, and illogical verse.
    ISBN: 0-9709443-4-9 (hbk. : alk. paper)
    1. Ostrich Logic—Juvenile literature. [1. Animals. 2. Verse. 3. Illustration.] I. Title.

Manufactured in the United States of America
1 2 3 4 5 6 – JR – 08 07 06 05 04 03

OSTRICH

An ostrich whose logic is a bone
of contention should never be told
to stand at attention. An ostrich whose
logic will not stand correction cannot be
expected to offer affection. An ostrich
whose logic causes indigestion will knock
you down at the slightest suggestion.

Ostrich logic is not for the weak. It's
nothing to sneeze at, wheeze at, or wink.
Ostrich logic is a dreadful thing. It's worse
than a boat full of camels who sing.

I sat at a table with an ostrich and
a plateful of bagels and lox. Have you noticed
how atrocious an ostrich
who's ferocious can be at a time like this?

To describe such a scene would be
awfully mean, and besides I'm not that
outrageous. An ostrich who is able will
sit at the table and complain that its food
tastes like socks.

*Ostrich nachos are a tasty treat. You
put'em in your mouth and you eat, eat,
eat. Ostrich toes make really good stew,
you put'em in your mouth and you
chew, chew, chew.*

As you can see, I'm certainly free
to discuss ostrich logic as I see it.
Make no mistake, I'm done with this
topic. I'm the expert of choice on this
subject of logic. But an ostrich with logic
will get the last word, it won't let us go
without being heard.

"I'm a first violinist and an abstract
expressionist, I'm an ostrich with
interest in a cucumber sandwich.
I'm a master mechanic and a maker
of magic. I'm a Renaissance ostrich
with a doctorate in logic."

CAT

This is a cat that has nine lives.

I know a cat that has nine cloves.

It seems to have a nose for the cloves it grows.

I know a llama who ate nine olives.

It lived in Oklahoma but moved to the Bahamas.

'Twas the llama's dilemma, the move to the Bahamas,

but it's happier now, it's the cat's pajamas.

DOG

A city dog

A dirty city dog

A gritty dirty city dog

A nitty gritty dirty city dog

Not a pretty witty giddy city dog

Not a silly celebrity dog from Cincinnati.

Ooh whah, ooh whah, doo whah ditty,

I'm talkin' 'bout the dog from New York City.

TORTOISE

A tortoise is never as curious or pompous as a porpoise
but is industrious instead. A tortoise has purpose, not like
a house mouse, but more like a hippopotamus.

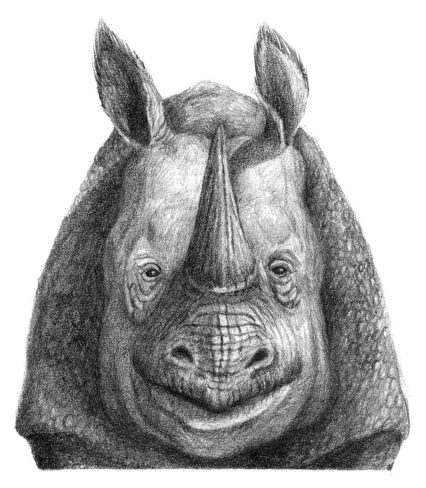

RHINOCEROS

Here's what a rhinoceros is not: A rhinoceros is not
a hippopotamus or Swiss chocolate or a chocolate
kiss or a macadamia nut. A rhinoceros is smaller
than a Tyrannosaurus, which is no longer with us.
A rhinoceros is bigger than 'most everything else,
including a breadbox or Volkswagen bus.

WARTHOG

You can't use a warthog like a library card, a back yard, or lard. A warthog is about as big as a St. Bernard and larger than a halibut. It won't fit in your lunchbox.

You won't find a warthog asleep on a golf course, riding a racehorse, directing a task force, or cooking liverwurst. A warthog won't make a mountain out of a molehill, look a gift horse in the mouth, or dwell in the school of hard knocks. You won't find a warthog searching the skies, seeking signs of life in the universe.

CAMEL

Do not compare a mammal like a camel to a smoked mackerel or a bathroom towel. Nor should a camel be compared with a caramel or carnival, though a camel will travel well, unlike a farm animal. A camel is a dromedary. A dromedary has lasting memory and the ability to walk a long way with great energy.

CROCODILE

This is a crocodile, not an alligator, a cucumber, or a tomater.
A crocodile won't put the cart before the horse or change
horses in midstream or become president of the United States.
I don't mean to say that a crocodile shouldn't be president,
but it's evident that being president requires a certain amount
of order. A crocodile is rarely ever heard from and spends
a lot of time underwater, unlike a president who walks above
ground and is often fodder for broader disorder. A crocodile
will not bite off more than it can chew.

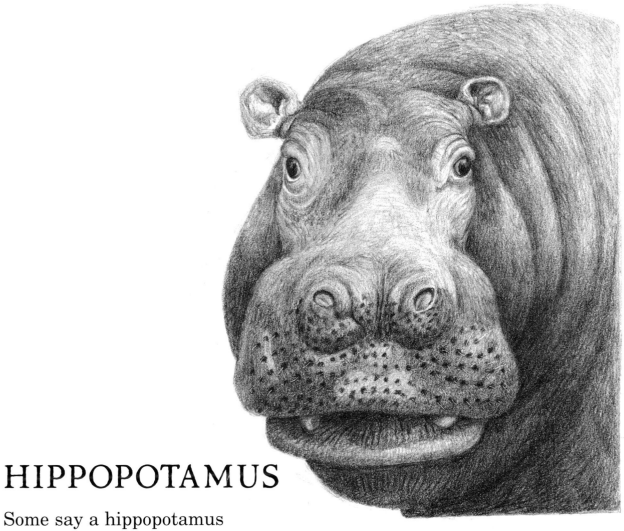

HIPPOPOTAMUS

Some say a hippopotamus
is dangerous, that it would
eat us. But I say ridiculous,
no need for nervousness,
it's not so monstrous.
I knew a hippopotamus,
it was never discourteous,
nor did it find me delicious.

RACCOON

Is this the raccoon
howled with a loon
they ballroom danced 'til noon?
Was that a spider, sat down beside her
by the light of a silvery moon? Was that the raccoon,
spider, and loon, they rode all night on a train?

Said the spider rider
to the raccoon beside her:
"Everything's brighter
when we dance to the music
from Spain, on a train, in the rain,
can't complain, don't explain, end refrain."

DOG

This is a sad soggy dog, not a fog or frozen yogurt or eggnog or sludge. Just a dog. Not a log or bog or furniture to lug or a frog or toad or load in the road or a crowd that's louder than a motor boater or roller coaster or carnival barker asking a quarter or more, why not a dollar?

This is a dog with a mug you could hug, who will sit on demand or give you a hand, or rather a paw, and wag a long tail without a care in the world and roll on the ground as would any good hound, then leap to her feet in an instant to greet with a tongue in your face 'til you back up and let out a holler.

This is a dog who will sleep or eat or round up sheep or come when she's called and that isn't all. When you walk she'll foller, there's no need to holler, 'cause the dog's a scholar of the highest order.

RABBIT

This is a rabbit, not a cabbage, not garbage, not a garage, or Alexander Graham Bell, who changed the world at large charging into the future with a mixture of fixtures to talk into and to listen to.

Hello? Hello?

FLAMINGO

A flamingo bo bingo sleeps all night long on long thin legs that are oh so strong. I met a flamingo who knew how to cook. It learned what it knew from a recipe book. It learned how to scramble, to broil, and to roast. It boiled some shoes, but it burnt the toast. We thank the flamingo, a gentle soul, for serving us lunch of flamed escargot.

TARSIER

This is a tarsier
not a thesaurus
or a Brontosaurus
or the Encyclopedia Britannica.
A tarsier is smallish
for us and would not be found
in Manitoba, Canada.

KOALA

This koala is quite dissimilar
from an umbrella
which it needs
in poor weather.
I read in a novella
about a koala
who loved the granola
at a cafeteria near Barcelona
where it sat at dinner with a gorilla
or maybe it wasn't Barcelona
it might have been Guatemala
but now I can't really rememba.

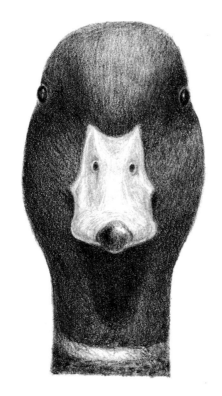

DUCK

A debonaire duck, my dear.
Not an apple or applesauce
or John Phillip Sousa.
Just a duck, not a pinto
bean or espresso machine or
picture postcard of Groucho Marx.
Not a pear or engineer or gondolier.
Just a duck, not a souvenir or fudge
or duck soup with gorgonzola
or the William Tell Overture,
that's for sure.

MOUNTAIN GOAT

This is a mountain goat, not a winter coat
or oats or a root beer float. This is the goat
that wrote about poets in sobering notes,
but worse than this is the following verse:

There once was a goat, cooked an octopus
roast and followed the feast with a yodel.
Three songs and a toast, sent everyone
home and declared: THIS ISN'T A HOTEL!

I have to go, but I'm glad we've met.
Please pardon my rush, I'm not upset.
I have to hurry and catch a jet
to visit the queen, Marie Antoinette.
She waits for me. You might suspect,
I'm her goat and a poet,
I'm her goat poet laureate.

PIG

This is a parsimonious pig.
Not a succulent swine
a hysterical hog
a sniveling sow
or a beastly boar.
You'd never mistake
a pig for a grocery store.

COW

Is this the cow with the cat
and the fiddle, the dish, and the spoon
that jumped clear over the moon?
Is this the cow that moved to New Jersey?
It's surely not lazy, it's rather busy.
Is this the Guernsey that moved
to New Jersey to be with a chimpanzee?
A little dog laughed to see such a flight
and a fish sang way out of tune.

COCKATOO

Please take note: Tonight, cockatoo will not be on the dinner menu. Instead, we bring you cheese fondue, lobster stew, broiled kangaroo, or creamed tofu, which tastes a lot like glue. Don't eat anything if you have the flu.

PANDA

This is a dancing panda, not an electric sander or sea
otter, peanut butter, bottle of water or portrait of my
daughter. I knew a panda and an otter and they
danced with a chair like Fred Astaire who danced a
dance in a house in France, or maybe it was Venice,
but it wasn't Minnesota.

GIRAFFE

A giraffe is tall rather than small, but all in all a giraffe with wings would be a better thing, although a giraffe with wings, of all things, would have a difficult time in a car. What's better by far than a giraffe in a car is a giraffe who simply says, "Please." A giraffe who's polite is a delightful sight as it reaches for leaves in the trees. That's when you see that a giraffe has knees, great pleasures to see, they're the bees' knees.

GIRAFFE

On behalf of the jesting jabbering chattering giraffe:
Don't laugh, cough, sniff, surf, or eat spaghetti sauce.
Do not linger, dawdle, or tarry. Be not idle or shiftless
and avoid sloths.

FROG

Ms. Suzy had a big frog
she named it Tiny Tim
she fed it tea and oranges
just to keep it trim.

Ms. Suzy had a small frog
she named it Giant Jim
she fed it peas and parsley
which always made it grin.

It jumped into the water
it jumped into the sea
it jumped into the Grand Canal
just to catch a flea.

A flea is not a baby
a flea is not a bird
a flea is not a hippo
that would be absurd.